CELLAR CELLAR CELLAR CELLAR
CELLAR CELLAR CELLAR CELLAR
CELLAR CELLAR CELLAR CELLAR
CELLAR CELLAR CELLAR CELLAR

Selected Anagrammatic
and Palindromic Micropoems

Anthony Etherin

Published by Penteract Press
Penteractpress.com
Penteractpress@gmail.com

Copyright © Anthony Etherin, 2018
anthonyetherin.wordpress.com
songsofinversion.com

FIRST EDITION

ISBN 978-1-9998702-0-1

The following leaflets by Anthony Etherin
are available from Penteract Press:

Wars of the Roses and Thorns
Palindrome-Sestina for Arnaut Daniel
The White Whale
Aelindromes
Mirror, Image
Luna Diffuses
Red Piano

CONTENTS

Frailty....................................1
Solemn....................................1
Control...................................1
The Trawler...............................2
Legend....................................2
The Tide..................................2
Song......................................3
The Mindful...............................3
Proverb...................................3
The Sea Nymph.............................4
Sirens....................................4
A Mermaid.................................4
Crows.....................................5
The City..................................5
Early Moon................................5
Conquering an Empire......................6
Wars of the Roses.........................6
Bastille..................................6
Beowulf...................................7
Alexander.................................7
Apocryphal Stories........................7

The River......................................8
Modern Prometheus........................8
Icarus..8
Sunset...9
Autumn..9
Harvest Moon.................................9
The Journey.................................10
The Forest...................................10
The Failed Cartographer..............10
Constrained Poetry.....................11
Buoyed...11
What is Poetry?...........................11
Exoplanet....................................12
Titan..12
Betelgeuse..................................12
Metaphors...................................13
Reverses.....................................13
Motifs..13
For Georges Perec......................14
Lost (On Cold Moors)..................14
Nitid Light....................................14

Mirrors..........................15
Madness.........................15
Rooms...........................15
Aelindrome in 1-2-1-2...........16
Aelindrome in 1-2-3-1-2-3.......16
Aelindrome in 1-2-3-4-1-2-3-4...16
Verge...........................17
The Sign........................17
Jest............................17
See Bees........................18
Chrysalis.......................18
Spider..........................18
Morning.........................19
Noon............................19
Night...........................19
Remembering.....................20
Merging.........................20
Arcadia.........................20
The Haunting....................21
Oh, Cellar!.....................21
Ghost Story.....................21

Mathematics of a Frozen Lake.......22
Crystals..........................22
Minerals..........................22
Tangled...........................23
Ad Astra..........................23
Stars.............................23
Questions and Answers.............24
Fall..............................24
Dreams............................24
The Gloaming......................25
The Mist..........................25
Midnight..........................25

A Note on the Constraints.........27
Acknowledgements..................29
Biography.........................31

for Clara

FRAILTY
Language has this frailty:
A hasty sunlight; a fragile
(largely aghast) faith in us....

SOLEMN
I sat, solemn.
I saw time open one poem.
It was in me, lost as I.

CONTROL
He cloned this short line's letters.
This led to other sentences, shrill
little notes in chords he shelters,
his teeth held in restless control.

THE TRAWLER

Trawl at sea, glared net.
Gull, listen:
Noon nets I'll lug--
tender algae stalwart.

LEGEND

Coasts share a legend:
Endless ages arch to a
dragon's scale--the sea.

THE TIDE

Evocate shore....
Dawn or evening,
I eroded its tips,
deltas at led spits.
Tide, do reign, in ever....
On, wader! Oh, set a cove!

SONG

Deep moonlight reveals
the older poems leaving
me, their pale song loved....

THE MINDFUL

Wonder....
By a radical plan,
my help met,
at serene rest,
a temple.
Hymnal, placid,
a ray bred now....

PROVERB

Once, it was said that
death is in two acts: A
cessation, with data,
and a white so static
it can eat its shadow....

THE SEA NYMPH

Dogma won.... I die.
Rendered now a siren,
I ramp mad atlases,
or speed a deep's rose salt.
A damp mariner is
a wondered nereid.
I, now, am God.

SIRENS

The outbound sirens,
eons hunted, orbit us,
but there is no sound....

A MERMAID

Nurse! So, hydrated,
a mermaid I am remade.
Tardy hoses run....

CROWS

The crows are back at the
weathercock that bears
a hawk. Both trace secret
arches to the backwater,
to caw at the brash creek.

THE CITY

Go flat, urbanised.
A cradle here held arcades
in a brutal fog.

EARLY MOON

Early, misty moon....
My solitary omen.
My rain looms, yet
it's only a memory.

CONQUERING AN EMPIRE

War!
Did I rule Rome?
No, no, troops!
In Italy, my Latin is poor to none.
More lurid, I draw....

WARS OF THE ROSES

Wars of the Roses--
Waste horses for
a fortress whose
sheets of arrows,
rash foes' towers
are sets, for show....

BASTILLE

Sir, a prison sum rots.
Due fatal war, Bastille fell.
It's a brawl at a feud.
Storm us?
No, sir-- Paris.

BEOWULF

Reading Beowulf,
I frowned. A bugle
blew a ruined fog.
"Go, run!" I fled a web--
fragile, unbowed....

ALEXANDER

Now raw,
Aristotle's severe hymn,
in us a palinode,
came to me--remote Macedon.
I lap a sun in my here vessel;
tot, sir, a war won.

APOCRYPHAL STORIES

Their apocryphal stories had
led a rich history to paper ash--
philosophies that dare carry
spherical Earth to dysphoria....

THE RIVER
In this feline noise,
revise river, thus sea.
I dream dark harm. Dead, raise us.
The river is ever, is none.
Life is thin.

MODERN PROMETHEUS
Refine research,
to see law,
then omen,
thaw,
else to char serene fire....

ICARUS
Cheap raise, toll fame....
Soar! Feathers aid you.
Cloudy airs heat, fearsome.
'Fall to sea!' I preach....

SUNSET

The autumn's wet with secret ghosts.
To get truths, we hatch its new muses.
We must watch this sunset together....

AUTUMN

Relapse, calm idyll....
Autumn, use sun mutually,
dim laces paler.

HARVEST MOON

The Harvest Moon is here.
This horseman over thee.
Heaven is her most other.
Shores move in the Earth.

THE JOURNEY
Dew.
A field, in alpine dales.
I rise, laden.
I plan.
Idle, if awed.

THE FOREST
In summer's white and yellow forest,
you find a new elm while storms rest.
Sun sets the memory in a wildflower.

THE FAILED CARTOGRAPHER
Demand a hill, at solid nadir....
Damn it!--
One morn, I saw I was in Rome,
not in Madrid,
and I lost all I had named.

CONSTRAINED POETRY
Constrained poetry:
Scan entropy, or edit
to read encryptions....

BUOYED
Trader, beg a sun robes us.
I manage,
buoyed away
by a wade you began....
A misuse, born usage, bred art.

WHAT IS POETRY?
What is poetry?
A wept history.
Pity, whose art
is atop the wry,
yet at worship.

EXOPLANET GJ-1132b

Sun, ever I flare....
Far, at some demo star: A
feral, fire Venus.

TITAN

Somewhere past Saturn:
Atmosphere. Raw sunset.
Rust ore. Ethane swamps.

BETELGEUSE

We dwarf Orion,
as a trap's knit elixir--
tall, ebb rose, resorb Bellatrix.
I let inks part,
as a **noir** of raw dew.

METAPHORS

Their poem reads itself:
Its form is peeled earth;
the tired, false promise
of time; the reader's lips.
Metaphors slide it free....

REVERSES

Trades reverses revere....
Hot, we fade lines I ran.
Words drown.
Arisen, I led a few to here--
verses' reversed art.

MOTIFS

The infinite forms
of inner time shift
in the finer motifs....

FOR GEORGES PEREC

Deft bed, test sentence.
Repel, lest sell, E, Perec!
Net, nest-set, debt fed....

LOST (ON COLD MOORS)

From snow-roots to moors--
so on, to tomorrow's forms--
sorrow's moot, frost moon....

NITID LIGHT

Timid, I tin it.
I sign it.
Filth? Gild it.
Insipid, it is.
I sit. I dip.
Is nitid light lifting?
I sit in it. I dim it.

MIRRORS
The Hall of Mirrors:
A horror fills them--
this roar from hell....

MADNESS
Peel song, no sadness.
Send a made bed a madness.
Send a song no sleep.

ROOMS
See turmoil in rooms:
more onerous limits,
more timorous lines....
Interior muses loom,
lost in our memories.

AELINDROME IN 1-2-1-2...
This art's sand,
a stem we posit.
Bricks crib its poem.
We stand as stars hit.

AELINDROME IN 1-2-3-1-2-3...
Deny me her ether, seven times.
A star I fly truly far is tamest--
I never see the rhyme end.

AELINDROME IN 1-2-3-4-1-2-3-4...
Moon--
Blinking a space,
I tag random ennui,
to ruin omen,
and grace its pagan ink, in bloom.

VERGE

Remove life's page.
Leave grief's poem.
I'm a verge of sleep.
Please forgive me.

THE SIGN

Red, nude pools,
eyed as a gem or a fallen king,
I saw a sign.
I knell a far omega--
sad eyes looped under....

JEST

Joyous reflections
justify cooler ones.
So, recount life's joy--
jest on, ferociously.

SEE BEES
See both silk cities.
Pill, eye no honey ellipse.
I, ticklish to bees....

CHRYSALIS
A shy echo splinters
those shiny parcels.
The chrysalis opens
physical otherness....

SPIDER
Spider, spider,
up to no saga,
so not pure,
dips,
re-dips....

MORNING
Nature painted this morning
as a thorn in untried pigment,
a mad night in turpentines, or
the turning points in a dream....

NOON
No one lit a love song
or petal,
up in a mist serene--
less astral arts,
as Selene rests,
I manipulate,
prognose
volatile noon....

NIGHT
Oh, instead paint gloom:
At night, some old piano.
A pained, moonlit ghost.
The dim sonata pooling
a poem in light and soot....

REMEMBERING
A mar on a past pure--
today can its bones irk.
Risen obstinacy (a dot)
erupts a panorama.

MERGING
More needless writing,
more winter seedlings--
entire worlds seeming
to merge in wilderness....

ARCADIA
Sun--
It so laid a cradle I faded,
light obeyed airy maxims' noise.
Low, to go, two lesions mix
a myriad eye both gilded:
A field Arcadia lost in us....

THE HAUNTING
Because man forgets how to die,
we become fine ghosts, our data
but echoed afterimages--So, now,
come out, beget fear in shadows....

OH, CELLAR!
Oh, cellar! Evoke
esoteric ire, to seek,
overall, echo....

GHOST STORY
I find your strange ghost
out in the fog, in dry grass--
grief haunts dying roots.

MATHEMATICS OF A FROZEN LAKE

Slam ice, dynamic.
A bad loch. Cold abaci--
many decimals....

CRYSTALS

Crystalline,
tiny cellars
silently arc--
try cells in a
lyrical nest.

MINERALS

Stibnites or onyx
or peridot ore.
Tin. I rag agates.
I set a gagarinite.
Rot, o dire proxy!
No rose. Tin bits.

TANGLED

Tangled hues of red
fold the sun, agreed
under the false god
of a gentle shudder.

AD ASTRA

Art, sad as me, opt
for odes I've devised, or, oft,
poems ad astra.

STARS

Stars in the sky--
Thirsty snakes.
Sky sirens that
skin the satyrs.

QUESTIONS AND ANSWERS

Answer the question,
to remember always
that those with truths are stronger.
But--
Stronger are truths
with those that always
remember to question the answer....

FALL

We are lost rivers, dried by fall.
(Leaves summer, to us, weary trees.)
Trees weary us to summer. Leaves
fall by dried rivers. Lost are we....

DREAMS

Dreamed I, where stars
were blues and greens,
those dreams of death,
the death of dreams....
Those greens and blues
were stars, where I dreamed....

THE GLOAMING

Those same early evening fogs that
soften the years save the gloaming.
Gone to mists, feathery leaves hang
in the heavy, agglomerate softness,
on the vines--meagre, ghostly as fate.

THE MIST

Emote no glee.
Fill its miasma or timid fog.
A rag of dim, it roams, aims
till I feel gone to me....

MIDNIGHT

Lawless midnight forever composes
verse from compelling shadows. I set
scenes from the improvised gallows,
the slow, simple coverings of dreams.

A NOTE ON THE CONSTRAINTS

CELLAR presents a selection of the anagrammatic and palindromic micropoems I have been sharing in my Twitter feed over the past two years. Most fit into one of two categories: Poems whose lines are perfect anagrams of each other, and poems that are palindromic by letter.

Also included are a number of poems that employ alternative styles of palindromism: Page 8 features "palindromes by pairs", or "two-letter-unit palindromes", while page 16 presents three "aelindromes"--a variation of my invention, which produces palindromes whose units of palindromism vary according to premeditated sequences (e.g. the phrase "melody, a bloody elm", which is palindromic in 1-2-3-4, since $(m)_1(el)_2(ody)_3(a\ blo)_4$ reflects backward as $(a\ blo)_4(ody)_3(el)_2(m)_1$.) Finally, page 24 features three word-unit palindromes.

This edition of CELLAR was typed using a restored 1930s' Imperial typewriter.

ACKNOWLEDGEMENTS

This small book is dedicated to my wife, Clara Daneri, whose support has meant and continues to mean everything to me.

I also owe debts of gratitude to many new friends and colleagues in the poetry and small press communities: My favourite poet, Christian Bök; Derek Beaulieu at no press; Ken Hunt at Spacecraft Press; Kyle Flemmer at The Blasted Tree; and Joakim Norling at Timglaset. Thanks also to Penn Jillette, Tanya Peixoto, and Pedro Poitevin for their support, as well as to all past contributors to Penteract Press, and to my expanding community of friends on Twitter.

30

Anthony Etherin is a UK-based writer of constrained, formal, and experimental poetry. His poems have appeared online in numerous publications, including Nagari, The Account and Cordite Poetry Review. He has had leaflets published by no press, Spacecraft Press, Timglaset, and The Blasted Tree, as well as by Penteract Press, which he runs, with his wife, Clara Daneri. He is on Twitter @Anthony_Etherin and archives his work online at anthonyetherin.wordpress.com.